PUBLICATIONS OF THE
AMERICAN INSTITUTE OF MUSICOLOGY

ARMEN CARAPETYAN
Director

BISHOP SMITH'S PART-SONG BOOKS

BY

JOHN P. CUTTS

MISCELLANEA

4

JOHN P. CUTTS

ROGER SMITH, HIS BOOKE

BISHOP SMITH'S PART-SONG BOOKS IN CARLISLE CATHEDRAL LIBRARY

AMERICAN INSTITUTE OF MUSICOLOGY

1972

INTRODUCTION

At long last it is possible to do something like justice to Bishop Smith's MS. Part-Song Books whose history has been chequered indeed. Two MS. Part-Song Books, Altus, and Bassus, now housed in the library of the Chapter of Carlisle Cathedral, were the subjects of interesting articles by James Walter Brown in *The Cornhill Magazine* for 1920-1921,[1] into whose possession they had most fortuitously come. He had received them in February 1917 from a widow of a friend with a letter saying 'I found the enclosed among my husband's books, and thought they might be of interest to you. If so, please keep them; if not, burn them.' Brown remembered his friend claiming to have bought them from an old book-stall (he couldn't remember exactly where, but he thought it was in Edinburgh), and realizing how narrowly they had escaped destruction determined that their proper home was the "Bodleian library in Oxford, where they were copied and 'sowne together' nearly 300 years ago." In the Bodleian they would then be readily accessible to students rather than in the Chapter library of Carlisle Cathedral where he had first thought of placing them, and where they might easily suffer from days of transition in which the continued existence of Deans and Chapters was itself precarious.

The part-books never got to the Bodleian: they are indeed in the Cathedral library at Carlisle. By kind permission of the Cathedral Chapter I have been provided with a complete microfilm of the two part-books, and am now presenting their first systematic detailed description after a preliminary investigation has revealed that they do contain materials that to the best of my knowledge have not proved extant elsewhere.

Apparently Brown held on to the part-books personally for some time, judging from a note pencilled in the manuscript itself to the effect that he sent the MS. books "to D^{r}. E. H. Fellowes/13th. March 1924" and "Received them back/31 May 1924," and also from his

[1] James Walter Brown, "An Elizabethan Song-Cycle," *The Cornhill Magazine*, XLVIII (1920), 572-9; "Some Elizabethan Lyrics," *The Cornhill Magazine*, LI (1921), 285-296.

statement that "Dr. E. H. Fellowes, who is a leading authority on the music of the period, has examined the books, and is unable to identify the composers of about thirty of the songs" (p. 285). These MS. books contain settings of several songs from the plays of John Fletcher (Brown himself in his first article had claimed that 'two of them' were by John Fletcher (p. 573) but did not identify them), and Fellowes himself brought out a few years later[2] an edition of whatever musical settings of songs from the plays of Beaumont and Fletcher that he could find supplementary to Lindsey's[3] list. It is strange that Fellowes did not avail himself of the settings "Arme, arme, arme, arme, ye scoutes are all come in" (Item 75-Altus Book) and "Orpheus I am come from the world below" (Item 74-Bassus Book), both from *The Mad Lover*, which up to that time had certainly not proved extant elsewhere, or of "Bring out yor conny-skins faire maides to mee" (Item 75-Bassus Book) from *Beggars' Bush* which at the moment of my writing has not proved extant elsewhere. If the settings had been in any way incomplete, uninteresting, or clearly negligible from a musical or dramatic point of view Fellowes' non-use of these materials would be understandable. But the two settings from *The Mad Lover* are extraordinary specimens of dramatic settings vastly superior in their attempt to be dramatic to almost every one Fellowes actually published. Both would have been a boon to scholars had their existence been known in the 1930s when scholars such as Lindsey were having to resort to the printed books of music of the late Seventeenth Century, which were by no means as rich in dramatic music for Fletcher's plays as these two Bishop Smith MS. part-song books. These *Mad Lover* settings did not come to light in other manuscript sources until many years later.[4] I have made the setting from *Beggars' Bush* the subject of a very recent article.[5] There is one other play song setting in the manuscript that I have been able to

[2] E. H. Fellowes, *Songs and Lyrics from the plays of Beaumont and Fletcher with Contemporary Musical Settings* (London, 1928).

[3] E. S. Lindsey, "The Music of the Songs in Fletcher's Plays," *Studies in Philology*, XXI, 2 (April, 1924), 325-355.

[4] See my *Musique de Scène de la troupe de Shakespeare 1604-1625*, (Paris, 1959).

[5] "A newly discovered early seventeenth-century musical setting of 'Bring out your cony-skins, fair maides, to me' from Fletcher's *Beggars' Bush*," *Comparative Drama*, v, 2 (Summer, 1971), 101-105.

identify, namely "Why so pale &c" (Item 68-Bassus Book) from Suckling's *Aglaura*.

Brown's main concern was to draw attention to what he called an Elizabethan song-cycle, a series of eleven songs ascribed to "R. Nicholson" whom Brown identified as Richard Nicholson, organist of Magdalen College, Oxford, January 1595/6 until 1639, and the first Heyther Professor of Music at Oxford appointed in 1626. Brown gave what he called a "condensation of the verses" which in point of fact amounted to the complete omission of verses 3, 5, 6, and 7, and a truncated version of 2. The whole text of 2 has been difficult to assemble since it needed a careful putting together of the various parts of the text distributed in both MSS. Brown described the music as written for three voices, of which "the triplex part, or melody, and the bass part are preserved" (p. 575). It would seem to me to be more correct to say that the cycle is scored for a treble (Altus Book) and a tenor (Bassus Book, but C Clef 4th line not F Clef). The group has no title in the MSS., but Brown's suggested title "John and Joane" is obviously appropriate. I present now for the first time the complete text of this secular song cycle, items 31-41 (both Altus and Bassus).

"John and Joane"

1

Joane quoth John when will it bee;
tell mee when wilt y^{u} marry mee:
my cow'fer and my calfe & rent,
my land is thine & tenement.
say Joane, say Joane what wilt y^{u} doe,
I cannot come euerie day to wooe.

Variant:
[2 mee when] mee Joane when Bassus

2

Ah silly John surpriz'd with ioy,
for ioy did make John silly,
ioy to enioy his sweetest Joane,
as white as any lilly,

alas I loue alas I loue
y^{t} loue y^{t} faile's mee neuer,
I loue y^{t} loue y^{t} loues my loue
& loue will mee for euer

yor loue is life, your life is blisse,
or blisse expresse of pleasure,
your loueing life & liueing loue
yeelds blisse aboue all measure.

oh loue is life oh life is blisse
god grant it so bee euer
wee cannot mend wee may doe worse
God grant it so bee neuer

her haire is faire as fairest gold
y^{t} kings in crownes doe weare
for faire & fairest is y^{t} gold
y^{t} is most like her haire

who's faire? 'tis Joane, who's kind? 'tis Joane,
'tis Joane surmounts ye sky,
who's cleare? 'tis Joane, but who doth loue?
ô god 'tis Joane & I.

Variants:

3 sweetest] whitest Bassus; 4 as white] Joane white Bassus; 9-12 omitted Bassus; 13-16 omitted Triplex; 18 in] on Bassus

3

That I loue Joane my glorie is,
yt shee loue's mee my treasure:
yt I loue her, & shee loues mee,
my mirth & heauenly pleasure.
Juno all wealth, Pallas all witt
belongs to y^{ee} alone,
all beauty Venus belongs to thee,
& I belong to Joane.

4

Cease ioyes, let downe yor strings of musicke layes,
admit a rivall now of dolefull mone;
cast downe ye myrtle twine & crownes of bayes,
& learne of mee to sorrow for my Joane.
ah Joane is sicke & vext with mickle paine;
God sheild my Joane, & send her well againe.

5

Liuest y^{u} John, is Joane forgot?
Joane y^{t} gaue y^{ee} ioyes in liueing:
liue no more, since Joane liue's not,
life to y^{ee} discomfort giueing.
ôh my ioyes of life are fled,
oh my Joane my Joane is dead.

6

Eyes henceforth lament your sight,
seing y^{t} your too much seeing
made you loue y^{t} heauenly wight,
being y^{t} shee is not beeing.
Joane is dead whom yow adore;
close your lids & see no more.

7

Thought, where are sweet fancyes now,
fancies humouring so to please thee:
Joane is dead y^{t} taught y^{ee} how
thinkeing fancies so to ease thee,
thought, since I must dye for thee,
leaue to thinke & follow mee.

8

Muse, ô canst y^{u} still indite,
Joane is dead & y^{u} dost know it:
Joane is dead y^{t} gaue y^{ee} light,
Joane y^{t} made y^{ee} first a poett,
tell ye world y^{r} dayes bee night,
say but so, & cease to write,
oh my ioyes of ioyes are fled,
oh my Joane my Joane is dead.

9

Banish sad sighes ye rest of restlesse greefe:
hence banish teares eue's dropping of my loue.
Joane is reviu'ed, Joane y^{t} sends releife,
to her poore John, her fellow turtle doue.
twist vp yor strings sweet Muses sing a straine,
to glad Johns poore hart, Joane is reviue'd againe.

10

Care for thy health, sweet Joane, as pearle of price:
care for thy John as hee care's much for thee.
let not each seaming good thing y^{ee} entice,
to hazard y^{t} w^{c}h should thine hono^{r} b^{ee}.
Kissing & culling is flame-catching fuell,
locke vp ye casket of thy cheifest iewell.
raddish & turnups (Joane) forbeare to eate:
bagpipes & bellowes are but windie meate.

11

John be contented & care not for mee:
I cannot, I will not bee ruled by thee.
Kissing & culling is louers delight;
y^{n} say w^{t} y^{u} will (John) for Joane will haue right.
Radish & turnups (John) ladies loue well,
though bagpipes & bellowes bee windye & swell:
John if yo^{w} loue mee, as loue yo^{w} require,
come kisse mee & cull mee, such death I desire.

As Brown pointed out, the MSS. are unusual, too, in containing a series of psalms set for three voices by Henry Lawes, items 45-49 (both Altus and Bassus). Each item separately numbered in the MSS. is subscribed "H. L.," and the last concludes with the flourish: "H. L. finis/Finis. Henry Lawes./Henrie Lawes./finis./." What Brown did not know, however, is that all fifteen of the Psalms are the paraphrases of George Sandys which had first been published in 1636,[6] and are carefully chosen to form a homogeneous unit, in the nature of a psalm cycle, or nascent oratorio.

Psalm: 31 [First stanza]

1 Who trusts in y^{ee} ô let not shame deject,
y^{u} euer just my chased soule secure;
Lord lend a willing eare with speed [bee y^{u} my rocke] ⌜protect,⌝
⌜be thou⌝ my rocke with thy strong arme immure.

Psalm: 57 [First stanza]

2 O y^{u} from w^{m} all mercy springs,
compassionate my sufferings:
& pitty mee
who trusts in thee:
ô shelter w^{t}h thy shady wings,
Vntill these stormes of woe
cleare vp :||: :||: or ouer blow.

Psalm: 38 [First stanza]

3 Not in thy wrath against mee rise,
nor in thy fury lord chastise:
thy arrowes wound
nail'd to ye ground,
thy hand vpon mee lyes, thy :||: :||:

[6] See K. E. Schmutzler "George Sandys' Paraphrases on the Psalms and the tradition of metrical psalmody: an annotated edition of fifty selected psalms, with critical and biographical introduction" (unpublished Ph. D. Dissertation, Ohio State University, 1956; there is no *music* given in the dissertation); Hallett Smith "English Metrical Psalms in the Sixteenth Century and their Literary Significance," *Huntington Library Quarterly*, IX (May, 1946); Virginia M. Lowell "English Metrical Paraphrases of the Bible 1549-1696" (unpublished Ph. D. Dissertation, University of Illinois, Urbana, 1947). The Carlisle MS. was unknown, of course, to all three.

Psalm: 60 [First stanza]

4 Cast off & scatter'd in thine ire,
lord on o^{r} woes, on :||: w^{t}h pitty looke,
y^{e} land's inforct found$\overline{\text{aco}}$ns shooke,
whose yawninge ruptures sighes expire:
ô curse y^{e} breaches y^{u} hast rent,
& make her firmely pmanent.

Psalm: 26 [First stanza]

5 Lord iudge my cause, thy peirceing eye
beholds my soule's integrity.
how can I fall
w^{n} I & all
my hopes on y^{ee} relye, when I :||:

Psalm: 142 [First stanza]

6 With sighes & cryes to God I prayd,
[I prayd] ⌜to him⌝ to him my suppli$\overline{\text{cao}}$n made:
power'd out my teares
my cares & feares
my wronges before him laide. my :||:

Psalm: 54 [First stanza]

7 Lord for thy promise sake defend,
& thy allsauing sheild, and :||: extend
ô heare my cryes, ô :||:
w^{c}h with wett eyes
& sighes to y^{ee} ascend, & :||: & :||: to thee ascend.

Psalm: 120 [Stanzas 5, 6]

8 Woe is mee y^{t} I from Israel

exiled must in Mesech dwell,
& in ye tents in ye tents of Ismaell.
ô how long, ô :||: shall I liue with those,
whose sauage minds sweete peace oppose,
& fury by diswasion growe's, by :||: &

Psalm: 5 [First stanza]

9 To heare mee lord be y^u incline'd
my thoughts ô ponder in thy mind,
& let my cryes acceptance find:
y^u hear'st my morneing sacrifice
to y^{ee} before ye daystarre rise
my prayers ascend, :||: ascend with stedfast eyes.

Psalm: 67 [First stanza]

10 Lord shower on vs thy grace,
enrich, enrich with gifts diuine:
let thy illustrious face
Vpon thy servants shine.
y^t all below
ye arched skye
may‸ ⌜thee⌝ & thy
salvation know thy salvation know.

Psalm: 13 [First stanza; part of second]

11 How long ô Lord, how :||: let mee not
for euer bee forgott, let :||: euer bee forgott.
How long, :||: my god wilt y^u
contract thy clouded brow, contract:||:
how long in mind perplext,
shall I bee daily vext

consider & heare my cryes,

illuminate my eyes,
lest with exhausted breath
I euer sleepe in death, I :||: I :||: in death.

Psalm: 71 [First stanza of Part *3*]

12 Now in ye winter of mine age, of :||:
When time hath snowe'd vpon my haires
hath snowe'd vpon my haires, vpon :||:
abandon not ô lord,
till I vnto this age p claime
thy mighty power, :||: thy power, till :||: thy mighty power in songs,
in songs ye same vnto ye next record.

Psalm: 2 [First stanza]

13 How are ye Gentiles all on fire
why rage they with vaine menacings,
earthe's‸ ⌜haughty⌝ potentates & kings
'gainst god and 'gainst his Christ conspire.
breake wee (say they) their servile bands
& cast their cords, & :||: from our free hands.

Psalm: 102 [First stanza]

14 Accept my prayers nor to ye crye
of my affliction stop thine eare.
lord in ye time of misery
& sad restraint serene appeare.
ye sighings of my spirit heare
& when I call with speed replye.

Psalm: 136 [First stanza]

15 The bountye of Jehouah prayse,
this God of gods all scepters swayes:

thankes to y[e] lord
of Lords afford,
& his amazeing wonders blaze:
for from y[e] king of kings
eternall mercye springs.

The MS. books, as presently constituted, indicate an attempt to set down at least eight series of songs for the first six of which the scribe used a new numbering. At the front of the Bassus Book the scribe began an index, viz:

3. Voc. pag: 1

1. A Sea- Nymph. pag: 1.
2. The Coblers wife. p. 2.
3. I liue, & yet. p. 3.
4. Fower armes. pag. 4, & 5.
5. O dulce mia Clori. pag: 5.
6. As fayre as morne. p. 6.
7. Wee happy heardsmen. p. 8.
8. Doe but consider. p. 8.

4. Voc. pag: 21

1. The death of Stephen. p. 21.
2. Mounseour Mingo. p. 22.

2. Voc. pag:

1. Sleepe, sleepe. pag:
2. Good folke. p.
3. I pray thee leave. p.

The same information is given at the beginning of the Altus Book with the addition of "3. Lady when I behold. p. 24." under the 4-voice section, and the omission of the 2-voice section altogether.

For the most part these divisions run according to the voice scoring which changes from three voices to four, to five, to three, and to two. In drawing up these lists I have indicated the divisions by the use of double lines.

Much confusion could result from considering these MS. books, Altus and Bassus, as indicating these voice ranges only. Although the word Altus is written at the top of many leaves in the Altus Book, the music is frequently scored for other voices. The same is true of the Bassus Book. In order to obviate difficulties, therefore, I have indicated in each case the Clef that has been used.

Both MSS. books carry the same list of contents for the first 63 items except for the inclusion of "The de‸⌜a⌝th of Stephen" (now strangely missing from the Bassus Book though clearly intended to be there according to the MS. index) in the Altus Book which I have taken the liberty of numbering 20a rather than 21 in order to preserve the close-listing correspondence between both MSS. Beginning with item 64 both MSS. are entirely different in contents and indeed it is these items (64-76 Altus; 64-75 Bassus) that constitute the main significance of the MSS. apart from the extraordinary secular and sacred song cycles in the earlier parts of both MSS.

There is clearly one handwriting throughout the manuscript with peculiar idiosyncrasies. The scribe's "v", with its ascending flourish, very frequently looks larger than what one would expect of the usual lower case. The peculiar use of apostrophe in a comparative, e.g., "highe'r" for "higher" (see Bassus Item 67) would seem to be an indication of an attempt at showing one syllable rather than two. Inside the end cover of the Bassus Book there is a list of books at the left hand side:

> Rec. by Mr Edmondson
> Leather cover'd bookes.
> Weelkes Fa la's 5 Bookes.
> Weelkes Fantastikes 3 Bookes.
> Byrd's lat. songes MS. 5 Bookes.
> Oriana's 6 Bookes
> Este's 5 Bookes, y^{e} first sett =
> Pietro Phillipi 8 Bookes.
> A MS. 5 Bookes.
> Stephano Venturi 5 Bookes.
> Horatio Vecchi 5 Bookes.

Hieronymus Praetorius 8 Bookes.
A MS. 4 Bookes in Octavo.
Bird & Tallis lat. songes 6 Bookes.
Holbornes, two Bookes.

On the right there is further information about books (3 entries possibly), but the handwriting is so faint that all I can make out for certain is "Books of Wilbys" and "Bird & Tallis."

I give now a complete listing of both MSS., followed by a detailed commentary. Brown printed several of the poetic texts in his article in 1920-21, though taking extraordinary liberties with the texts, silently expanding some contractions while correctly maintaining others, altering lower to upper case and altering punctuation, but since these are now difficult to come by I have decided to give the texts again and also for the sake of completeness.

Lists of Contents of Bishop Smith's Part-Song MS. Books

Altus
Bassus

Bishop Smith's Song Books — so-called Altus Book

Item	MS. No.	MS. Pagin-ation	Part Scoring	First line	How written out despite the fact that Altus figures at the top of many leaves.	
1	1	[1]	3 Voc.	A Sea-Nymph sate vpon yᵉ shore	Treble G Clef	5 staves
2	2	[2]	3 Voc.	The Coblers wife of oʳ towne	Treble G Clef	4 staves
3	–	bottom of [2]	3 Voc.	Now wee are mett, &c. (no more words here but more in Bassus)	Treble G Clef	1 stave
4	3	[3-4]	3 Voc.	I liue, & yet methinkes I do not breath	C Clef 1st line	6 staves head attr. "Wilby"
5	4	[4]	3 Voc.	Fower armes, two neckes, one wreathing	Treble G Clef	3 staves head attr. "Weelkes"
6	5	[5]	3 Voc.	O dulce mia Clori, o Clori mia bella	C Clef 1st line	2 staves
7	6	[6-7]	3 Voc.	As faire as morne, as fresh as may	C Clef 1st line Medius at top of [6-7]attr."Wilby"	8 staves
8	7	8	3 Voc.	Wee happy heardsmen here, may singe & eke reioyce	C Clef 2nd line	2 staves
9	8	8	3 Voc.	Doe but consider this small dust	Treble G Clef	3 staves attr. "Alf. Ferabosce"
		9		Extra verses to "Wee happy heardsmen &c." at top Latin verse "Perspicuus vitro" subscribed "Hier: Amalthus, | alias HE" at bottom.		
		10		Blank — bearing impressions of verses on p. 9		

Item	MS. No.	MS. Pagin-ation	Part Scoring	First line	How written out despite the fact that Altus figures at the top of many leaves.	
10	9	11	3 Voc.	Gloria Patri et filio et Spiritui sancto	C Clef 3rd line	4 staves attr. "Rich: Deering"
11	–	11	3 Voc.	fa la la :||: (no more words)	C Clef 3rd line	1 stave
12	10	12	3 Voc.	Springtime mantleth euery bow	C Clef 2nd line Triplex at top	5 staves attr. "Morley"
13	[11]	13	3 Voc.	Iô to Hymen :||: to Hymen sing aloud	C Clef 1st line Triplex at top	4 staves
14	[12]	14	3 Voc.	Tell mee (Deare) faine would I know	C Clef 1st line Triplex at top	4 staves
15	[13]	15	3 Voc.	Welcome sweet pleasure	Treble G Clef Triplex at top	4 staves
16	[14]	16	3 Voc.	Come pritty wagg & sing	C Clef 1st line Triplex at top	3 staves attr."Mart:Pearson"
17	[15]	16-17	3 Voc.	Sing loue is blind, & so is loue's lady	Treble G Clef Triplex at top	3 staves
18	[16]	17	3 Voc.	To pitch our toyles go we	Treble G Clef Triplex at top	3 staves
19	[17]	18	3 Voc.	Then wth reports most sprightly	C Clef 1st line Triplex at top	2 staves
20	[18]	18	3 Voc.	What need ye Sun to shine	Treble G Clef Triplex at top	3 staves

Item	MS. No.	MS. Pagin-ation	Part Scoring	First line	How written out despite the fact that Altus figures at the top of many leaves.	
		19		Blank — bearing impressions of music not present in MS.		
		20		Blank — bearing impressions of music not present in MS.		
20a	1	21	4 Voc.	The de‸⌜a⌝th of Stephen (no more words)	C Clef 3rd line	4 staves
21	2	22-23	4 Voc.	Mounsieur Mingo for quaffing doth passe	C Clef 3rd line	8 staves
22	3	24-25	4 Voc.	Lady when I behold, :||: ye roses sprouting	C Clef 1st line	8 staves head attr. "Wilby"
		26-27		Missing altogether		
23	5	28	4 Voc.	No words given	C Clef 3rd line	2 staves
		29		Blank — has a very faint copy of music on it of item 24 "Sweete Jesu"		
		30		Blank — has impression of item 23 on it		
24	6	31	4 Voc.	Sweete Jesus helpe ô helpe	C Clef 2nd line	4 staves
25	7	32-33	4 Voc.	When as I glance :||: on my louely Phillis (completed at foot of p. 33. Pointing hands at foot of pp. 32 and 33 clearly indicate)	Treble G Clef	6 staves head attr. "Bennet"
26	8	33	4 Voc.	Cruell vnkind, my heart y^u^ hast bereft mee	C Clef 1st line	4 staves head attr. "Bennet"
27	9	34	4 Voc.	O sleepe, :||: ô sleepe fond fancy	C Clef 3rd line	5 staves head attr. "Bennet"

Item	MS. No.	MS. Pagin-ation	Part Scoring	First line	How written out despite the fact that Altus figures at the top of many leaves.	
28	10	35	4 Voc.	Woe is mee :||: y^{t} I Im constrained to dwell	C Clef 3rd line	4 staves head attr. "Child"
29	11	36-37	4 Voc.	O stay faire cruell, doe not still torment mee	C Clef 1st line	7 staves head attr. "Este"
30	12	38-39 40	4 Voc.	O bone Jesu, o dulcissime Jesu Blank — with impressions of p. 39 (last 2 staves of item 20)	C Clef 4th line	7 staves
31	1	41	3 Voc.	Joane quoth John when will it bee	C Clef 1st line Triplex at top	4 staves attr."R.Nicholson"
32	2	42-43	3 Voc.	Ah silly John :||: surpriz'd with ioy	C Clef 1st line Triplex at top	8 staves attr."R.Nicholson"
33	3	44	3 Voc.	That I loue Joane my glorie is	C Clef 1st line Triplex at top	4 staves attr."R.Nicholson"
34	4	45	3 Voc.	Cease ioyes, let downe yor strings	C Clef 1st line Triplex at top	4 staves attr."R.Nicholson"
35	5	46	3 Voc.	Liuest y^{u} John, is Joane forgot?	C Clef 1st line Triplex at top	3 staves attr."R.Nicholson"
36	6	47	3 Voc.	Eyes henceforth lament your sight	C Clef 1st line Triplex at top	3 staves attr."R.Nicholson"
37	7	48	3 Voc.	Thought, where are sweet fancyes now	C Clef 1st line Triplex at top	3 staves attr."R.Nicholson"

Item	MS. No.	MS. Pagin-ation	Part Scoring	First line	How written out despite the fact that Altus figures at the top of many leaves.
38	8	49	3 Voc.	Muse, ô canst y^{u} still indite	C Clef 1st line 4 staves Triplex at top attr."R.Nicholson"
39	9	50	3 Voc.	Banish sad sighes ye rest of restlesse greefe	C Clef 1st line 4 staves Triplex at top attr."R.Nicholson"
40	10	51	3 Voc.	Care for thy health, sweet Joane	C Clef 1st line 5 staves Triplex at top attr."R.Nicholson"
41	11	52-53	3 Voc.	John be contented & care not for mee	C Clef 1st line 6 staves Triplex at top Finis.|R.Nicholson.|Finis.|
		54-59		Missing altogether	
42	1^{a} pars	60	5 Voc.	Ne irascaris Domine satis	C Clef 3rd line 4 staves Medius at top head attr. "Byrd"
42a	2^{a} pars	61	5 Voc.	Civitas sancti tuj	C Clef 3rd line 4 staves Medius at top head attr. "Byrd"
43a (See Bassus)	4th part (5.)	62-63	5 Voc.	Were I a bird how would I fly	C Clef 4th line 6 staves back to Altus at top attr. "Phillips"

Item	MS. No.	MS. Pagin-ation	Part Scoring	First line	How written out despite the fact that Altus figures at the top of many leaves.	
44		64-65	5 Voc.	Goe Phoebus, goe, wee care not for thy brightnes	C Clef 3rd line	6 staves
		66		Blank — with impression of p. 65 (last 2 staves of item 44)		
		67-68		Missing		
45	1	69	3 Voc.	Who trusts in y^{ee} ô let not shame deject	C Clef 1st line Cantus 1^{mus} + "Psal:31" at head "attr. H.Lawes"	3 staves
46	2	70	3 Voc.	O y^{u} from w^{m} all mercy springs	C Clef 1st line Cantus 1^{mus} + "Psal:57" attr. "H.L."	2 staves
47	3		3 Voc.	Not in thy wrath against mee rise	C Clef 1st line Cantus 1^{mus} + "Psal:38" attr. "H.L."	2 staves
48		71	3 Voc.	Cast off & scatter'd in thine ire	C Clef 1st line Cantus 1^{mus} + "Psal:60" attr. "H.L."	3 staves
49	5	72	3 Voc.	Lord iudge my cause	C Clef 1st line Cantus 1^{mus} + "Psal:26" attr. "H.L."	2 staves

Item	MS. No.	MS. Pagination	Part Scoring	First line	How written out despite the fact that Altus figures at the top of many leaves.
50	6		3 Voc.	With sighes & cryes to God I prayd	C Clef 1st line 2 staves attr. "H.L."
51	7	73	3 Voc.	Lord for thy promise sake defend	C Clef 1st line 3 staves Cantus 1mus + "Psal:54" attr. "H.L."
52	8	74	3 Voc.	Woe is mee yt I from Israel	C Clef 1st line 3 staves Cantus 1mus + "Psal: 120 v:4,5,6./ attr. "H.L."
53	9	75	3 Voc.	To heare mee lord be yu incline'd	C Clef 1st line 3 staves Cantus 1mus + "Psal:5./" attr. "H.L."
54	10	76	3 Voc.	Lord shower on vs thy grace	C Clef 1st line 3 staves Cantus 1mus + "Psal:67./" attr. "H.L."
55	11	77	3 Voc.	How long ô Lord, how :||:	C Clef 1st line 5 staves Cantus 1mus + "Psal: 13./" attr. "H.L."
56	12	78	3 Voc.	Now in ye winter of mine age	C Clef 1st line 4 staves Cantus 1mus + "Psal:71./" attr. "H.L."
57	13	79	3 Voc.	How are ye Gentiles all on fire	C Clef 1st line 3 staves Cantus 1mus at head attr. "H.L."

Item	MS. No.	MS. Pagin-ation	Part Scoring	First line	How written out despite the fact that Altus figures at the top of many leaves.
58	14	80	3 Voc.	Accept my prayers nor to ye crye	C Clef 1st line 3 staves Cantus 1^{mus} at head attr. "H.L."
59	15	81	3 Voc.	The bountye of Jehouah prayse	C Clef 1st line 3 staves Cantus 1^{mus} at head attr. "Henry Lawes|"
60		82	3 Voc.	Rorate caeli, :||:desuper	Treble G Clef 4 staves Cantus 1.us at head attr. "A. Ferabosco, Junior"
61		83	3 Voc.	Halleluiah :||:	Treble G Clef 4 staves Cantus 1.^{mus} at head attr. "A. Ferabosco, Junior"
62		84-85	3 Voc.	O had not Venus been beguild'	C Clef 1st line 7 staves
63		86	3 Voc.	Hence Vaine affection, leaue mee,	C Clef 1st line 4 staves Cantus primus at head attr. "Mr Deering"
		87		Blank	
		88-91		Missing altogether	

Item	MS. No.	MS. Pagin-ation	Part Scoring	First line	How written out despite the fact that Altus figures at the top of many leaves.
64		92		Like to ye blaze of fond delight	C Clef 1st line with Bass 2 double staves
					Nothing at head except Versus 1.^{mus}
	93				1 double stave — "turne ouer to ye Chorus"
		94		(Euen such is man)	Chorus 1. C Clef 1st line (Treble) 2. C Clef 3rd line(Altus) 3. C Clef 4th line(Tenor) 4. Bass (Bassus)
		95			Versus 2 dus. — "turne ouer to ye Chorus."
		96		(Euen such is man)	Chorus (4 voices as on p. 94 above) attr. "Arth: Phillips."
		97		Blank — carries impression of some music not now present in MS.	
		98		Blank	
65		99	2 Voc.	My love & I for kisses played	G Clef 4 staves Treble at head — "ye Base in ye Tenor-booke"

Item	MS. No.	MS. Pagin-ation	Part Scoring	First line	How written out despite the fact that Altus figures at the top of many leaves.
66		100	2 Voc.	O tell mee tell thou God of wind	4 staves Treble at head — "ye Base in ye Tenor-booke"
67		101	2 Voc.	He y^t^ in heauen with Seraphins will sing	Treble G Clef 3 staves followed by Bassus one stave with only "Hee that in heauen, &c." underlaid. Nothing at head of page
68		102	2 Voc.	I made a couenant with my heart	Treble G Clef 4 staves Treble at head
		103		I made a couenant with my heart	Bassus at head 3 staves only incipit "I made a couenant, &c.|"
69		104	2 Voc.	Fyer, :||: lo here ⌜I burne⌝ in such desire	G Clef 4 staves Treble at head attr. "Nicholas Laneere"
		105		Fyer, :||: lo here ⌜I burne⌝ in such desire	Bassus at head 3 staves only incipit "Fyer, fyer, &c.|" attr. "Nicholas Laneere"
70		106	2 Voc.	Gently gently prithee time,	G Clef 4 staves Treble at head
		107		Gently gently prithee time,	Bassus at head 3 staves only incipit "Gently, gently, &c.|"

Item	MS. No.	MS. Pagin-ation	Part Scoring	First line	How written out despite the fact that Bassus figures at the top of many leaves
71		108	2 Voc.	O greife, :||: how diuers are thy shapes	Nothing at head of page except "To King James Vpon ye death of Prince Henrie.|" Treble G Clef 3 staves Bassus 2 staves with incipit and 2nd stanza at foot.
72		109	2 Voc.	"'Tis now dead night, & not a light on earth"	Nothing at head of page except "To Queene Anne, vpon ye death of Prince Henrie.|" Treble G Clef 3 staves Bassus 2 staves and 2nd stanza at foot.
73		110 } 111 }		Words to "See ye building, &c." Second and third verses. Good impression of music of p. 109 on it. See ye b^uilding, wch whilest my Mistris liv'd in	Nothing at head Treble G Clef 3 staves Bassus 2 staves with incipit
74		112	2 Voc.	Thou sentst to mee a heart was crown'd	Treble G Clef 3 staves Bassus -1 stave with incipit Nothing at head 2nd stanza at foot

Item	MS. No.	MS. Pagin-ation	Part Scoring	First line	How written out despite the fact that Bassus figures at the top of many leaves
75		113-118	2 Voc.	Arme, arme, arme, arme, ye scoutes are all come in	Treble G Clef with Bassus Nothing at head 2 double staves each page "Finis, of ye Battle.|"
76		119		What's a Cuckold learne of mee	Treble G Clef 4 staves Bassus 2 staves with incipit Nothing at head
					so-called Bassus Book
1	1	1	3 Voc.	A Sea-Nymph sate vpon ye shore	C Clef 3rd line 4 staves
2	2	2	3 Voc.	The Coblers wife of our towne	C Clef 4th line 3 staves
3				Now wee are mett, lets merry merry bee	Bass Clef 2 staves
4	3	3	3 Voc.	I liue, & yet methinkes I do not breath	C Clef 4th line 5 staves head attr. "Wilby"
5	4	4	3 Voc.	Fower armes, two neckes, one wreathing	C Clef 2nd line 3 staves head attr. "Weelkes"
6	5	5	3 Voc.	O dulce mia Clori o Clori mia bella (top 3 staves on this page are blank but bear [as does the whole page] strong impressions of all 5 staves of p. 6)	Bass Clef 2 staves
7	6	6-7	3 Voc.	As faire as morne, as fresh as May	C Clef 3rd line 9 staves head attr. "Wilby"

Item	MS. No.	MS. Pagin-ation	Part Scoring	First line	How written out despite the fact that Bassus figures at the top of many leaves	
8	7	8	3 Voc.	Wee happy heardsmen here	Bass Clef	2 staves
9	8		3 Voc.	Doe but consider this small dust	Bass Clef	3 staves attr. "Alf. Ferobosco"
		9		Extra verses of item 8 "Wee happy heardsmen," and Latin version of item 9 "Perspicuus vitro pulvis" subscribed "Hier: Amaltheus,|alias HE."		
		10		Blank — impressions of verses of p. 9		
10	9	11	3 Voc.	Gloria Patri et Filio et Spiritui sancto	Bass Clef	4 staves attr. "Rich: Deering"
11		11		fa la la :||: (no more words)		
12	10	12	3 Voc.	Springtime mantleth euery bow	C Clef 4th line	5 staves attr. "Morley"
13		13	3 Voc.	Iô to Hymen :||: to Hymen sing aloud	Bass Clef	4 staves
14		14	3 Voc.	Tell mee (Deare) faine would I know	C Clef 4th line	4 staves
15		15	3 Voc.	Welcome sweet pleasure	Bass Clef	3 staves
16		16	3 Voc.	Come pritty wagg & sing	Bass Clef on *3rd* line	4 staves attr. "Martin Peirson"
17		16-17		Sing loue is blind, & so is loue's lady	Bass Clef on *3rd* line	3 staves
18		17	3 Voc.	To pitch our toyles go wee	Bass Clef	3 staves
19		18	3 Voc.	Than with reports &c. (no more words)	Bass Clef	2 staves attr. "Th. Wilkinson"

Item	MS. No.	MS. Pagination	Part Scoring	First line	How written out despite the fact that Bassus figures at the top of many leaves	
20		18		What need ye morning rise, &c. (no more words)	Bass Clef	3 staves
		19		Blank — impression of p. 20 on it		
21		20-21	4 Voc.	Mounseour Mingo for quaffing doth passe	Bass Clef	8 staves
22	3	22	4 Voc.	Lady, when I behold, ye roses sprouting (looks incomplete but it is quite clear that an unmarked repetition beginning "whether ye roses" should go back to the middle of stave 4)		
		23		Blank — bears impression of next page		
23	5	24	4 Voc.	No words given	Bass Clef	2 staves
		25		Blank — very faint music of "Sweete Jesus helpe" (see item 27)		
		26		Blank — impression of some music on it		
24	6	27	4 Voc.	Sweete Jesus helpe ô helpe sweete Jesus	Bass Clef on 3rd line	4 staves
25	7	28-29	4 Voc.	When as I glance, :||: on my louely Phillis	C Clef 3rd line	6 staves head attr. "Bennet"
26	8	29	4 Voc.	Cruell vnkind, my heart thou hast bereft mee	C Clef 3rd line	4 staves head attr. "Bennet"
27	9	30	4 Voc.	O sleepe, ô sleepe fond fancie	Bass Clef	5 staves head attr. "Bennet"

<table>
<tr><th>Item</th><th>MS. No.</th><th>MS. Pagin-ation</th><th>Part Scoring</th><th>First line</th><th>How written out despite the fact that Bassus figures at the top of many leaves</th></tr>
<tr><td>28</td><td>10</td><td>31</td><td>4 Voc.</td><td>Woe is mee, :||: y[t] I am constrained</td><td>Bass Clef 4 staves
head attr. "Child"</td></tr>
<tr><td>29</td><td>11</td><td>32-33</td><td>4 Voc.</td><td>O stay faire cruell doe not still torm[t] mee</td><td>Bass Clef on 3rd line 7 staves
head attr. "Este"</td></tr>
<tr><td>30</td><td>12</td><td>34-35
36</td><td>4 Voc.</td><td>O bone Jesu. |o dulcissime dulcissime Jesu
Blank — clear impression of p. 35</td><td>Bass Clef 6 staves</td></tr>
<tr><td>31</td><td>1</td><td>37</td><td>3 Voc.</td><td>Joane, quoth John when will it bee</td><td>C Clef 4th line 4 staves
attr. "R. Nicholson"</td></tr>
<tr><td>32</td><td>2</td><td>38-39</td><td>3 Voc.</td><td>Ah silly John :||: surpriz'd with ioy</td><td>C Clef 4th line 8 staves
attr. "R. Nicholson"</td></tr>
<tr><td>33</td><td>3</td><td>40</td><td>3 Voc.</td><td>That I loue Joane my glorie is</td><td>C Clef 4th line 4 staves
attr. "R. Nicholson"</td></tr>
<tr><td>34</td><td>4</td><td>41</td><td>3 Voc.</td><td>Cease ioyes, let downe your strings</td><td>C Clef 4th line 4 staves
attr. "R. Nicholson"</td></tr>
<tr><td>35</td><td>5</td><td>42</td><td>3 Voc.</td><td>Liue'st y[u] John, is Joane forgott?</td><td>C Clef 4th line 3 staves
attr. "R. Nicholson"</td></tr>
<tr><td>36</td><td>6</td><td>43</td><td>3 Voc.</td><td>Eyes henceforth lament your sight</td><td>C Clef 4th line 3 staves
attr. "R. Nicholson"</td></tr>
<tr><td>37</td><td>7</td><td>44</td><td>3 Voc.</td><td>Thought, where are sweet fancies now</td><td>C Clef 4th line 3 staves
attr. "R. Nicholson"</td></tr>
</table>

Item	MS. No.	MS. Pagin-ation	Part Scoring	First line	How written out despite the fact that Bassus figures at the top of many leaves
38	8	45	3 Voc.	Muse, oh canst y^{u} still indite	C Clef 4th line 4 staves attr. "R. Nicholson"
39	9	46	3 Voc.	Banish sad sighes, ye rest of restlesse greefe	C Clef 4th line 5 staves attr. "R. Nicholson"
40	10	47	3 Voc.	Care for thy health, sweet Joane	C Clef 4th line 5 staves attr. "R. Nicholson"
41	11	48-49	3 Voc.	John bee contented, contented, & care not for mee	C Clef 4th line 7 staves
		50		Blank — impression of p. 49	
		51		Blank	
		52-53		Missing altogether	
42	1^{a} pars 2	54	5 Voc.	Ne irascaris domine satis	C Clef 4th line 5 staves head attr. "Byrd"
42a	2^{a} pars	55	5 Voc.	Ciuitas sancti tuj	C Clef 4th line 5 staves head attr. "Byrd"
43	1st part	56-57	5 Voc.	Tell mee no more of pleasure (3rd, 4th, 5th verses underlaid)	Bass Clef 10 staves attr. "Phillips"

Item	MS. No.	MS. Pagination	Part Scoring	First line	How written out despite the fact that Bassus figures at the top of many leaves
44		58	5 Voc.	Goe Phœ bus, goe, wee care not for thy brightness (incomplete)	Bass Clef 5 staves
		59		Blank — very faint copy of item 45 on it	
		60		Blank — with impression of music (not now present in MS.)	
45	1	61	3 Voc.	Who trusts in yee ô let not shame deject	Bass Clef 3 staves attr. "H. Lawes"
46	2	62	3 Voc.	O yu from wm all mercy springs	Bass Clef "Psal:57" head [Ca] Bassus 4 staves attr. "H.L."
47	3	62	3 Voc.	Not in thy wrath against mee rise	Bass Clef "Ps:38" 2 staves attr. "H.L."
48	4	63	3 Voc.	Cast off & scatter'd in thine ire	Bass Clef "Psal:60" 3 staves attr. "H.L."
49	5	[58] 64	3 Voc.	Lord iudge my cause	Bass Clef "Psal.26" 2 staves attr. "H.L."
50	6	64	3 Voc.	With sighes & cryes to god I pray'd	Bass Clef 2 staves attr. "H.L."
51	7	65	3 Voc.	Lord for thy promise sake defend	Bass Clef "Psal:54" 3 staves attr. "H.L."

Item	MS. No.	MS. Pagination	Part Scoring	First line	How written out despite the fact that Bassus figures at the top of many leaves
52	8	66	3 Voc.	Woe is mee y^{t} I from Israell	Bass Clef "Psal:120,v. 4,5,6" 4 staves attr. "H.L."
53	9	67	3 Voc.	To heare mee lord bee y^{u} enclin'd	Bass Clef "Psal:5" 4 staves attr. "H.L."
54	10	68	3 Voc.	Lord shower on vs thy grace	Bass Clef "Psal:67" 3 staves attr. "H.L."
55	11	69	3 Voc.	How long lord, how long	Bass Clef 5 staves attr. "H.L."
56	12	70	3 Voc.	Now in ye winter of mine age	Bass Clef "Psal:71" 4 staves head [Cant] Bassus attr. "H.L."
57	13	71	3 Voc.	How are ye Gentiles all on fire	Bass Clef "Psal:2" 4 staves attr. "H.L."
58	14	72	3 Voc.	Accept my prayers nor to ye cry	Bass Clef "Psal:102" 3 staves attr. "H.L."
59	15	73		The bounty of Jehovah prayse	Bass Clef "Psal:136" 3 staves attr. "H.L." Finis Henry Lawes.|Henrie Lawes.| finis.|
60		74	3 Voc.	Rorate caeli, :||: desuper	Bass Clef 5 staves attr. "A. Ferabosco Junior"

<table>
<tr><th>Item</th><th>MS. No.</th><th>MS. Pagin-ation</th><th>Part Scoring</th><th>First line</th><th>How written out despite the fact that Bassus figures at the top of many leaves</th></tr>
<tr><td>61</td><td></td><td>75</td><td>3 Voc.</td><td>Hallelujah :||:</td><td>Bass Clef 4 staves
attr. "A. Ferabosco Junior"</td></tr>
<tr><td>62</td><td></td><td>76-77</td><td>3 Voc.</td><td>O had not Venus been beguil'd</td><td>C Clef 4th line 7 staves</td></tr>
<tr><td>63</td><td></td><td>78</td><td>3 Voc.</td><td>Hence vaine affection, leaue mee</td><td>C Clef 4th line 4 staves
attr. "Mr Deering"</td></tr>
<tr><td></td><td></td><td>79</td><td></td><td>Blank — clear from impressions</td><td></td></tr>
<tr><td></td><td></td><td>80-81</td><td></td><td>Missing altogether</td><td></td></tr>
<tr><td></td><td></td><td>82</td><td></td><td>Blank — clear from impressions</td><td></td></tr>
<tr><td>64</td><td></td><td>83</td><td>2 Voc.</td><td>Sleepe, sleepe, though greife torments thy body</td><td>Bass Clef 5 staves
head — "Bassus.|ye Treble in ye Cantus-booke"</td></tr>
<tr><td>65</td><td></td><td>84-85</td><td>2 Voc.</td><td>Good folke for loue or hyer</td><td>Bass Clef 6 staves
head — "Bassus.|ye Treble in ye Cantus-booke"</td></tr>
<tr><td>66</td><td></td><td>85</td><td>2 Voc.</td><td>I pray thee leaue, loue mee no more, &c. (no more words)</td><td>Bass Clef 2 staves
head — "Bassus.|ye Treble in ye Cantus-booke"</td></tr>
<tr><td>67</td><td></td><td>86-88</td><td>2 Voc.</td><td>Away to ye fountaine you y^{t} will refine</td><td>C Clef 4th line 12 staves
attr. "Arth:Phil:"
head — "Bassus ye Treble is in ye end of ye Tenor-booke.|"</td></tr>
</table>

Item	MS. No.	MS. Pagination	Part Scoring	First line	How written out despite the fact that Bassus figures at the top of many leaves	
68		88	2 Voc.	Why so pale &c. (no more words)	Bass Clef head — "Bassus.|ye Treble is in ye end of ye Tenor-booke."	2 staves
69		89	2 Voc.	Great & proud, if shee deride mee	Treble G Clef Bassus — 2 staves	3 staves
70		90	2 Voc.	Faire in a morne ô fairest morne	Treble G Clef Bassus — 2 staves	3 staves
71		91	2 Voc.	Woods, rockes & mountaines	Treble G Clef Bassus — 2 staves	3 staves
72		92	2 Voc.	Now I see thy lookes were faigned	Treble G Clef Bassus — 2 staves Stanzas 3, 4 at foot	2 staves
73		93	2 Voc.	O your louely sparklings eyes	Treble G Clef Bassus — 1 stave	2 staves
74		94-95	2 Voc.	Orpheus I am come from ye depths below	Treble G Clef Bassus — 3 staves	7 staves
75		96-97	2 Voc.	Bring out yor conny-skins faire maides to mee	Treble G Clef Bassus — 3 staves	7 staves
		98		"For ye Base Viole" — scales and "Tuneinge" and a Bass line — 1 stave		
		99		"for ye Base Violl" "Tuninge"		
		100		Vocal exercise on vowels and scales	C Clef 3rd line	3 staves

NOTE

Throughout the Commentary the following abbreviations have been used to facilitate reference work:

EMV E. H. Fellowes, ed. *English Madrigal Verse* (Oxford, 1920 [rep. 1950]).

FLIEP Margaret Crum, ed., *First-Line Index of English Poetry 1500-1800 in Manuscripts of the Bodleian Library*, Oxford, 2 vols. (Index Committee of the Modern Language Association of America), 1969.

:||: is the manuscript's way of indicating a repeat common in Sixteenth and Seventeenth-Century music MSS.

Commentary

Item 1 I have not found this item elsewhere. Brown's edition of the poetic text (p. 290) did not record the MS. corrections and repetitions:

> A Sea-Nymph sate vpon ye shore,
> while Dio drown'd came floating to her
> a fisher whom she long had lov'd before.
> Dio alas Alas shee sung. Alas [my] poore Dio:
> harke how ye winds, harke how ye winds sigh
> as they fly [‸⌜sigh⌝] as they fly ‸⌜sigh⌝ as they fly.
> ye while ye beaten rockes they cry,
> & broken murm [e] ⌜u⌝ rs of ye sea sadly reply.
> Dio o Dio alas, Alas poore Dio, Alas poore Dio,
> Alas poore Dio:
> Dio, o Dio alas, Alas, Alas poore Dio, Alas, Alas poore Dio./

The episode recalls Ceyx and Alcyone (*Metamorphoses*, XI). The musical setting with its long drawn out lament and reiterated play on "Dio" suggests similarities with the songs performed by the choir boys of St. Pauls and of the Chapel Royal (see G. E. P. Arkwright "The Death Songs of Pyramus and Thisbe," *Notes & Queries*, tenth series V (May 5, 1906), 341-3, and V (May 26, 1906), 401-3; "Early Elizabethan Stage

Music," *Musical Antiquary*, I (October 1910-July 1911), 30-40, IV (October 1912-July 1913), 112-117; "Elizabethan Choirboys' Plays and their Music," *Proceedings of the Royal Musical Association*, XI (1913-1914), 117-138.

Item 2 I haven't found this item elsewhere. Brown printed the poetic text (p. 295) omitting the refrain and repetitions:

> The Coblers wife of o^r towne
> Hath beaten her good man.
> Wherew^t hall?
> With an Aull
> & an Elson threed;
> fa la la la la la fa la la la la la la la la la la.
>
> She knockt ye knave about ye head,
> She knockt ye knave about ye head,
> She made his nose to bleed.
> fa la la la la la la fa la la la la la la
> fa la la la la fa la la la la.

Item 3 This was printed in *The Musical Companion*, 1673 with music ascribed to Simon Ives, and is included in Bodleian Library MS. Mus. d. 8, ff. 26^v, 27. It is not included in the index of this Carlisle Cathedral manuscript, but since it occurs at the foot of the folio in both Altus and Bassus Books, it could have been added after the index had been entered. The handwriting is identical with the rest of the manuscript.

> Now wee are mett, lets merry merry bee,
> for one halfe howre wth mirth & glee,
> to recreate our spirits dull,
> lets laugh & sing our bellyes full.

[See FLIEP N.592.]

Item 4 This is printed in John Wilbye's *The Second Set of Madrigales To 3. 4. 5. and 6. parts, apt for both Voyals and Voyces*. 1609, vii-viii There are no variants from the text as given in *EMV*, p. 239.

Item 5 This is the first stanza only of item XIV in Thomas Weelkes' *Ayeres Or Phantasticke Spirites for three voices*. 1608. There are no variants from the text as given in *EMV*, p. 227 save for the fact that fa la la refrains occur at the end of each couplet, and

Fellowes omitted them by design. Also included in Christ Church Music MS. 439, f. 4^{v}.

Item 6 I have not traced this:

O dulce mia Clori,
O Clori mia bella,
o chara mia stella
Speranza decori,

Tu balma restori
la vita mi daie

io solo mi stracco
mi strugo mi faccio.

o Clori mia bella
o Clori :||:
O :||:

Item 7 Printed in John Wilbye's *The Second Set of Madrigales*... 1609 as number V. (See Item 4 above.) There are no variants from the received text in *EMV*, p. 239 save for the fa la la refrains designedly omitted by Fellowes and for the inclusion in line 8 of "Ah," before "She frowns."

Item 8 This was the first item printed by Brown (p. 286) from these manuscripts after his truncated version of the "John and Joan" cycle. Brown called it a Christmas carol. To my mind it recalls the shepherds' song in *The Taylors & Shearmens Pageant* "As I out rode this enderes night—Doune from heav ē from heaven so hie" (see "The Second Coventry Carol...," *Renaissance News*, X, 1 [1957], 3-8 for text and music), and may well have belonged to a similar dramatic entertainment. It is quite clear that the text itself suggests movement from the place where the shepherds heard the voice of angels to the journey itself as they trudged to Bethlehem, and on to the very place of Christ's birth.

Wee happy heardsmen here,
may singe & eke reioyce;
for angells bright & cleare,
wee saw, & heard their voice.
Wee saw & heard their voice.

Glad tidings they vs told;
y^{e} king of all mankind
is borne & in cloathes fold;
They say wee may him find.
They say wee may him find.

In Bethlehem in a stall,
& eke his mother free:
Glad tidings to vs all;
Yea blessed may hee bee.
Yea blessed may hee bee.

Come let vs all $w^{t}h$ ioy
in heart to Bethleem trudge:
To see y^{t} blessed boy,
$w^{c}h$ once must bee o^{r} judge
$w^{c}h$ once must bee o^{r} judge.

All Haile ô Christ our kinge"
All Haile ô virgins sonne;
wee pray thee vs to bring,
In Heauen wth y^{ee} to wonne.
In Heauen wth y^{ee} to wonne.

Where wee y^{e} Father may
See $w^{t}h$ y^{e} Holy ghost:
& glorifye alway
Him y^{t} of might is most.
Him y^{t} of might is most.

Item 9 This, printed as No. VIII of *The Under-Wood* in Jonson's 1640F, has been the subject of a recent detailed study by Edward Doughtie "Ferrabosco and Jonson's 'The Houre-Glasse'," *Renaissance Quarterly*, XXII. 2 (Summer, 1969), 148-150. Doughtie corrected Brown's guess that the subscription of the Latin verse (on the back, not facing, however, as Doughtie says) — "Hier: Amaltheus|alias HE" referred to Henry Edmondson, a college acquaintance of Smith's, by pointing out that the Latin verse, Jonson's source, "was composed by Giolamo Amaltei, and was originally printed in Ramutius Gherus' (*i.e.*, Janus Gruterus') *Delitiae* cc *Italorum Poetarum* (1608), I, 73" — information stemming basically from C. H.

Hereford, Percy and Evelyn Simpson, eds., *Ben Jonson*, (Oxford), XI (1950), 53. Doughtie gives the text of "Doe but consider this small dust" with MS. abbreviations expanded and modern typographical conventions followed, and also the text of "Perspicuus Vitro pulvis qui dividit horas." [See FLIEP C.695, D.353.]

Item 10 The doxology has a vigorous musical setting. Deering repeats "et Spiritu sancto" once and "et in sæcula sæculorum amen" once and concludes with "sæculorū amen, sæculorum A-men."

Item 11 This "fa la la :||:" consists of only one line. Since it is not numbered separately in the MS., presumably it was added later but it is in the same handwriting and pen as the rest. It is not part of or an extension of the fa la refrain of the next item:

Item 12 This was printed as number xxiv in Thomas Morley's *Canzonets or Little Short Songs to Three Voyces*, 1593. There are the following variants from the text as given by Fellowes in *EMV*, p. 125, not counting the fa la la refrain which Fellowes designedly omitted:

2 bowers] bowes; 5 shepherd's] Virgin's; 6 true love are] Love shall be.

Item 13 I have not traced this hymeneal elsewhere: Brown did not print it.

Iô to Hymen sing aloud
delitious pleasures now grow proud.
Now Venus blesse ye nuptiall bed,
Wherein is lost a maidenhead,
is lost alas & gott wth play
wth many a pish & fy away.

Item 14 John Hilton's *Ayres, Or, Fa las For Three Voyces*, 1627 included this as number xiii. There is only one variant from the received text as printed by Fellowes in *EMV*, p. 102, namely "you" for "we" in line 4.

Item 15 This was printed in Thomas Weelkes' *Ballets And Madrigals*, 1598, as number xv. Only the first verse is given here in the MS. Fellowes indicates in *EMV*, p. 216 the existence of a "Fa la la" refrain at the end of each stanza, but does not give a "no no no" refrain at the end of the fourth line as is here the case in the MS.

Item 16 Martin Peerson included this as number xv in his *Priuate Musicke*, 1620. There is only one variant from the received text in *EMV*, p. 164, namely "pleasant" for "dainty" in line 5. Number xvi in Peerson's *Priuate Musicke*, Part 2, occurs as Item 19 in this MS.

Item 17 This is number xviii from Peerson's *Private Musicke*. The text is so different from that printed in *EMV*, p. 164, that it is worth quoting in full here.

Sing loue is blind,
& so is loue's Lady, yet in ye darke
loue light can find.
Cupid want's Eyes & is a Baby,
ô no, |. |. though Cupid's blind & younge w^{t}hall,
yet he will make ye strongest fall,
wth a hey nonny :| |: no .|. w^{t}h a .|. hey .|.

Item 18 I have not traced this elsewhere, but occurring as it does in the middle of a group of Martin Peerson's settings may possibly indicate that this setting is his too. It is all the more suggestible in that its style and treatment of the themes — green woods' hunting — are similar:

To pitch our toyles go we,
w^{t}h mirth & merry glee,
bowes are bent w^{t}h arrowes keen,
for ye forrest green:
up goe's ye deer & in ye wood she flingeth
y^{t} w^{t}h ye Echo all ye forrest ringeth,
hornes & beugles blow
Chanter Chanter ho,
there boyes there boyes ho,
they cry they cry so ho.

Item 19 This is the second part (of which Item 16 is the first part) with Martin Peerson's setting as printed in *Private Musicke*, 1620, number xvi. The setting is different from that for the first part. The Bassus Book strangely carries the attribution "Th. Wilkinson." There are the following variants from the received text as printed in *EMV*, p. 164:

3 So wittily] omitted; 6 sound] ground altered to "sound."

Item 20 The Altus Book has this lyric beginning with the third line of what was printed as number xix in Peerson's *Private Musicke*. The Bassus Book has merely the words of the first line "What need ye morning rise, &c." Obviously in this duet between two lovers alternative lines were meant to express the separate sentiments of both parties. The Bassus Book makes it clear that the Bass started, but since it gives no more of the poetical text all that can be reported are variants from the received text (*EMV*, p. 165) in such lines as are apportioned to the Triplex:

3 a] the; 12 Let no hate] ô let no fate.

Item 20a A second series of items begins with this — it is strangely missing from the Bassus Book.

Item 21 This is a welcome addition to the settings already known to be extant (see my "Some incidental music newly discovered for *2 Henry IV*," *Shakespeare Quarterly*, VII, 4 (Autumn, 1956), 385-393, and Sternfeld, F. W., "Lasso's Music for Shakespeare's 'Samingo'," *Shakespeare Quarterly*, IX, 2 (Spring, 1958), 105-116). There are so many important variants from the text as given in *Shakespeare Quarterly*, VII, 4 (Autumn, 1956), particularly in the use of different repeats, that it merits printing here *in toto*, especially in view of its importance for *2 Henry IV*. There are so many silent editorial emendations in the text given by Brown (p. 294) that I have thought it wiser to give the text again and in full:

Mounsieur Mingo for quaffing doth passe
Bassus] Mounseour
[&] ⌜in⌝ cup, cruse, can, or glasse;
in celler never was
his fellow found,
to drinke profound
by tap, & turne so round:
to drinke, carrowse so sound,
& doth beare so fresh a braine, Bassus] yet beares
saunce staint or straine, staint or straine
of foule recoill or quarrell

but to ye good beare barrell,
where hee workes to winne his fame:
& stout doth stand
in Bacchus band
with a pott in his hand
to purchase fame,
hee calls come off for shame,
& try my cunning man to man;
& let him conquer mee y^t can:
I care not,
nor spare not
whilst hand can heaue ye pott,
no feare falls to my lott, Bassus] omits the repeat
no feare falls to my lott.
Good Bacchus doe mee right
& dub me knight
Don Mingo.

[See FLIEP M. 448-449]

Item 22 This was printed as number x (and again as xxiv) in John Wilbye's *The First Set of English Madrigals*, 1598. There is one possible variant from the received text as given in *EMV*, p. 234, namely "double, double" in line 4 for just "double" — a repetition which is consistently given and may not simply be a musician's license.

Item 23 — No words

Item 24 I have not traced this item elsewhere. Brown does not print it. Its pleading for one drop of mercy recalls Faustus' plea.

Sweete Jesus helpe ô helpe
sweete Jesus helpe sweete Jesus helpe.
helpe a mournefull spirit, a mournefull spirit.
my sins as ye sands ye sands in number in number
pressing my soule my soule:
one droppe, one droppe, one droppe, one droppe
one droppe of mercy sweete lord Bassus] good Lord

Item 25 This was printed as number x in John Bennett's *Madrigalls to Foure Voyces*, 1599. There are no variants from the received text as given in *EMV*, p. 25 unless the Altus manuscript's use of "wth roses & with lillies" the first time is not simply musician's license for the received text "with roses and lillies." The Bassus uses "roses and lillies" each time.

Item 26 Number xi in John Bennet's *Madrigalls To Foure Voyces*, 1599. There are no variants from the received text as printed in *EMV*, p. 25.

Item 27 Number xii in John Bennet's *Madrigalls To Foure Voyces*, 1599 was printed in Thomas Morley's *A Plaine and Easie Introduction to Practical Musicke*, 1597, Sig. Bb. 6ᵛ. There are the following variants in both Altus and Bassus Books from the received text as given in *EMV*, p. 26:

1 head] head alas; 3 I say, and] I say, fond fancy, and. [See FLIEP 0788 — does not note Bennet]

Item 28 This metrical version of only verse 5 from Psalm 120 is different from that included later in the MSS. Song Books for verses 5 and 6 as number 8 in a series of 15.

Woe is mee :||: y^{t} I am constrained to dwell,
y^{t} :||: :||: to dwell
wth Mesech, to :||: & to haue my habitation,
and to :||: among ye tents of Kedar, Kedar,
among :||: among :||: Kedar.

Item 29 Printed as number ix in Michael East's *Madrigals to 3. 4. and 5. parts*, 1604. There are two variants from the received text as given in *EMV*, p. 75: 3 doth lament] doth (now) lament (Altus only); 6 to spill] spill.

Item 30 This is quite different from the text used by Palestrina in his "O bone Jesu" — O bone Jesu! miserere nobis; quia tu creasti nos, tu redemisti nos sanguine tuo pretiosissimo.

O bone Jesu, o dulcissime Jesu,
o dulcissime dulcissime Jesu,
o dulcissime Jesu, o :||:
O Jesu, O dulcissime Jesu, O Jesu,
fili Mariæ Virginis, fili :||:
O dulcis Jesu, O :||:
secundum magnam misericordiam tuam.
secundum :||: O :||:
O dulcis Jesu, O :||: O :||:

O dulcissime Jesu, O dulcissime Jesu
O dulcissime dulcissime Jesu, O :||:

Items 31-41 This is obviously intended to be a separate unit in the manuscript with a new numbering. I have already giventhe texts of these in the introduction. The first item 31 occurs also in B. M. Add. MSS. 17786-91 ascribed to "Nikcolson" from which John Stafford Smith edited it for inclusion in *Musica Antiqua* (London, 1812), I. 32.

Item 42 Items 42, 42a, 43a, and 44 do not compromise a homogenous unit and it is hard to imagine how lost pieces possibly written out on pp. 67-68 now missing could have pulled this group together.

Items 42 and 42a are obviously parts of a Latin version of the Psaltery and were printed in William Byrd's *Cantiones Sacrae For Five Voices*, 1589, as nos. 20 and 21 respectively. (See W. Horsley, ed., *Cantiones Sacrae* (London, Musical Antiquarian Society, July 1842.)

Item 43a, 43a In the Altus Book only the 4th, 5th, and 6th stanzas are given: The Bassus Book gives the earlier stanzas. Brown printed the text (p. 291) expanding some abbreviations and modernizing some spellings. I have not traced the text elsewhere:

Tell mee no more of pleasure, I
do loath (it) such guilded misery,
shew mee ye place of grottes & cells,
or tell mee w^{r} Sylvanus dwells.

give mee some gloomy vault, whos site
was nee'r acquainted wth ye light:
y^{t} I may spend my future age
in some forsaken Hermitage.
Nothing but sorrow, cares, & feares,
well pickled in ye brine of teares,
shall be my meate & drinke; for these
displeasures now do onely please

Were I a bird how would I fly
from this disease of liberty:

then w^{t}h my best contriueing thought
I'de ly in ambush to be caught:
I'de court & wooe ye fowlers rage
to damme & blesse me to a cage:
I'd fall in loue w^{t}h fetters, this,
this blessed bondage were a blisse.

And since y^{t} my vnhappy breath,
make's mee but liueing in my death;
I'de fight w^{t}h snares, y^{t} in ye strife
I might be murderd into life.

Although divisions of the poetical text as it is underlaid are indicated by the use of numbers in parenthesis, i.e. (3.), (4.), (5.) all twenty lines of the text are through-set in the Bass, which would incline one to believe that the Altus Book at one time may also have shown the whole text through-set instead of starting with (4.). The present consecutive numbering of the pages in the MS., of course, gives no indication that other pages may have been lost from this section, and there is the more positive proof that no pages are lost here by the fact that p. 62 bears a remarkable impression of p. 61 — "Civitas sancti tuj."

Item 44 This item, printed in *Musical Companion*, 1673, pp. 206-7 and there with its musical setting ascribed to "Flecknoe" occurs also in Filmer MS. All a-e ff. 113^{v} (Canto), 113^{v} (Alto), 112^{v} (Quinto), 112^{v} (Tenor), 116^{v} (Basso) ascribed to "Mr. Flecknall." Since the text is not readily available to students of seventeenth-century lyrics I have decided to give it here:

Goe Phoebus, goe, wee care not for thy brightnes,
'tis ye Moone send's us home full of ioy & lightnesse.
By her wee dance, & lightly trip our measures,
till ye Nimphs & ye Faunes & ye Satyrs are fill'd wth pleasures:
by her wee sing, & sweetly tune our voices,
till ye hills & ye woods & ye rocks & ye floods and ye aire reioyce's

Items 45-49 This cycle of paraphrases of the Psalms has already been the subject of discussion in the introduction.

Item 60 The text is taken from *Isaiah*, 45.8:

> Drop down, ye heavens, from above,
> and let the skies pour down righteous-
> ness: let the earth open, and let them
> bring forth salvation —

Item 61 The text consists of only the word "Halleluiah" marked to be repeated nineteen times.

Item 62 Printed as number xii in John Hilton's *Ayres, Or, Fa las For Three Voyces*, 1627. There are no variants from the received text as given in *EMV*, p. 102 except for the inclusion of the fa la la refrains which Fellowes designedly did not print.

Item 63 I have not traced this item elsewhere:

> Hence vaine affection, leaue mee,
> thou cans^{t} no more with flattering hopes deceiue mee.
> May I liue but to see my wrongs repayed,
> my passed greife would quickly be allayed.

Item 64 James Walter Brown printed the text of this (p. 288), with some abbreviations expanded, as complete in twelve lines without indicating the manuscript's careful distinction between the verses. The words are underlaid for each of the four chorus parts: I give that of the top line, the Treble.

> Versus 1.^{mus} Like to ye blaze of fond delight,
> or like a morning cleare & bright,
> or like a frost, or like a shower,
> or like ye pride of Babell's tower,
> or like ye houre y^{t} guide's the time,
> or like to Beauty in her prime.
>
> Chorus Euen such is man, whose glory lend's
> his life a blaze or two, and end's.
>
> Versus 2 dus. Delights vanish, ye morne orecasteth,
> ye frost breake's, ye shower, hasteth,
> ye tower fall's, ye hower spends,
> ye beauty fade's, & man's life end's.
>
> Chorus Euen such is man, who liue's by breath.
> now here now there, :||: in life & death.

Brown considered that the last two lines "similar to lines 7 and 8 in the second and third stanzas printed as Wastell's in Mr. H. J. Massingham's 'Seventeenth Century Anthology of English Verse'" had evidently been tacked on by Arthur Phillips the composer to "round off his music." It would seem to me that the obviously deliberate attempt to set the different lengths of the two verses indicates more careful adherence to the text in front of him than casual exercise of musician's license. It may well be that the first section with chorus and the second section with chorus indicate careful division on something like the basis of the octave and the sextet respectively of the Italian sonnet, though of course the obvious scheme is too facile for either Elizabethan or Italian sonnet. Arthur Phillips was succeeded by Dr. John Wilson as Professor of Music at Oxford.

Item 65 This item was printed by Brown (p. 291) with some abbreviations expanded, with no recognition of William Strode's authorship (see Bertram Dobell, ed., *The Poetical Works of William Strode* (London, 1907), p. 47. The setting is by John Wilson and is extant in Wilson's *Cheerful Ayres* (Oxford, 1659), pp. 144-5 and in Bodleian Lib. MS. Mus.b.1. f.16^{v} (see *Musica Disciplina*, X (1956), 142-209, and 156 esp.) and in Edinburgh University Library MS. Dc.1.69, 81, f.45 (see *Musica Disciplina*, XIII (1959), 169-194 and 188 esp.).

Item 66 This item printed in *Wit Restor'd*, 1658, p. 97 is included by Bertram Dobell in his edition of Strode (see previous item) and attributed to him. Its juxtaposition in this MS. to an acknowledged Strode item would seem to me to support Dobell's attribution. FLIEP 0816 points out that the item is included also in Bodleian MS. Eng. poet, f.25, f.63^{v}.
[See FLIEP 0.816]

Item 67 Brown printed this item (p. 287) and silently modernized by expanding some abbreviations, capitalizing, and altering punctuation. For the sake of accuracy, since the text occurs nowhere else in print to the best of my knowledge, I give here the text in full:

He y^{t} in heauen with Seraphins will sing,
& beare a part in y^{r} sweet harmonie:
must here on earth touch David's warbling string,
& praise w^{t}h himmes ye sacred Trinitie.

for musicke is ye type of paradise,
Gods ioy, mans comfort, Angells exercise.

The music for the last two lines is marked for repeat. Brown considered these lines "worthy of being displayed in letters of gold in every choir vestry."

Item 68 Brown printed this item (pp. 292-93) which he considered superior to two other versions of the lyric printed by Robert. Jamieson in *Popular Ballads*, 2 vols. (Edinburgh, 1806), II 297-8 and II, 146-7, this latter being entitled "The Shepherd's Covenant with his own heart." Brown's editorial practice makes it necessary to give the text again here. The first verse is set apart in its music, each line given a separate line of music: verse 5 has a separate music for its first two lines; the third and fourth are underlaid under first and second. Verses 3 and 4 are written out under verse 2 which has a different part of the music from the beginning and from the end.

I made a couenant with my heart,
y^{t} it & I would neuer part,
till I should giue it to some one,
where it might euer lye alone.

and first a beauteous citty-face
meethought did promise such a grace.
but all was taken vp before,
and prentice writt vpon ye doore.

next sought I in a ladies brest,
voide (as shee told me) of a guest:
w^{r} in I found were diuers roomes,
for lords, for pages, knights & groomes.

& last a seeming country-maide
pffer'd it harbour and it stayed:
but ôh before ye moone grew old,
she for a toy her selfe had sold.

wearie'd with travaile & w^{t}h scorne,
home it return'd where it was borne.
now doth it seeke nor sue to none,

but here will liue & dye alone.

Item 69 This lyric was very popular. Two musical settings have survived, one by Campion and this one by Nicholas Lanier. See Walter R. Davis, ed. *The Works of Thomas Campion* (New York, Doubleday, 1967), pp. 156-158, pp. 497-498 for details of other versions extant. There are the following variants from the text given by Davis:

> 4 mine idle empty] my emptye louesicke; 6 *Trent*, and *Humber*, and fayre *Thames*] Humber, Trent & silver Thames; 7 Dread] dead: thy] yor; 11 hell] helpe; 12 backward] backwards; 13 And... his] omit... his; 15 then,] come; 17 save] salue; 18 That] w^{c}h.

Particularly important among these variants, because occurring nowhere else to the best of my knowledge are those in lines 7 and 13, and possibly in line 17 if "salue" is not (as it so frequently is in Renaissance MSS.) another spelling of "saue." [See FLIEP F.317.]

Item 70 This item is also extant in Ch. Ch. MS. Mus. 87, ff. 14^{v}-15 from which I printed it in *Seventeenth-Century Songs and Lyrics*, (University of Missouri Press, 1959), p. 120 and in "M^{ris} Elizabeth Dauenant 1624, Christ Church MS. Mus. 87," *RES*, X, 37 (February, 1959), 26-77, esp. 35-36, the latter version with all the repetitions of words, presumably due to musician's license. Bishop Smith's MS. has exactly the same repetitions of words, and only one variant, namely "there" for "them" in line 4.

Item 71 This and the next item are welcome additions to the many elegies occasioned by the death of Prince Henry in 1612. (A modern hand has added "in 1612" at the head of the page.) (See *EMV*, p. 207 for John Ward's *The First Set of English Madrigals to 3. 4. 5. and 6. parts apt both for Viols and Voyces. With a Mourning Song in memory of Prince Henry*, 1613. The elegy "In memory of Prince Henry" was the last number, xxviii, in that collection.
[See FLIEP A.1975, etc. under index of Prince Henry for numerous others.]

As far as I have been able to determine these two have not proved extant elsewhere:

To King James vpon ye death of
Prince Henrie

O greife, how diuers are thy shapes w^{r} in men languish?
ye face sometime w^{t}h teares y^{u} killst
with vnseene anguish.
Some while y^{u} smil'st
to veiw how fate,
playe's w^{t}h o^{r} humane state:
so farre fro surety here
are all o^{r} earthly ioyes,
y^{t} w^{t} o^{r} strong hope builds, w^{n} least wee feare
a stronger power destroye's

O fate, why shouldst y^{u} take from kings y^{r} ioy & treasure?
y^{r} image if men should deface
'twere death; w^{c}h y^{u} dost race,
euen at thy pleasure.
wisedome of holy kings yet knowe's
both wt it hath & owe's.
heauens hostage; w^{c}h though bred
& nurst with such great care:
it rauisht now great king, & from vs led,
w^{n} wee were least aware.

Item 72 To Queene Anne, vpon ye death
of Prince Henrie.

'Tis now dead night, & not a light on earth
or starre in heauen doth shine:
let now a mother mourne ye noblest birth
y^{t} euer was both mortall & divine
O sweetnes peerlesse, more y^{n} humane grace:
o flowry beauty, O vntimely death.
now Musicke fill this place
w^{t}h thy most dolefull breath.
O singing waile a fate more truely funerall,
y^{n} w^{n} w^{t}h all his sons ye Syre of Troy did fall.

Sleepe ioy, dye mirth, & not a smile bee seene,
or shew of harts content:
for neuer sorrow nearer toucht a queene,
nor were y^{r} euer teares more fitly spent.
o sad remembrance, full of ruefull woe;
o ceaselesse passion, o vntimely inhumane hower,
no pleasure now can grow,
for withered is her flower.
o anguish doe thy worst in furie tragicall:
since fate in taking one, hath thus disorder'd all.

Item 73 Brown printed this lyric (pp. 293-294) according to his usual practice of maintaining some abbreviations, silently expanding others, and silently altering lower case to upper case. He compared it wisely with an anonymous "Obsequies" included on p. 371 of Massingham's seventeenth-century anthology. See also Norman Ault's *A Treasury of Unfamiliar Lyrics* (London, 1938), pp. 154-5. The same words without music occur in B.M. Add. MS. 24665, ff. 78-78^{v}.

See ye building
w^{c}h [once] whilest my Mistris liv'd in,
  [those] was pleasure's essence:
see how it droopeth
and how nakedly it looketh
  without her presence.
harke how ye hollow wind doth blowe:
  & seeme to murmure,
  in euery corner,
    for her being absent;
from hence they chiefly grow:
    ye cause w^{r}fore I now
these sighes & sorrowes show.

See ye garden
w^{c}h I receaued reward in.
  for my true loue:
lo see those places,
w^{r} I inioye'd embraces
  y^{t} Gods might move
O see ye arbour w^{rin} shee

with melting kisses,
distilling blisses
through my fond lips,
with ioy shee ravisht mee,
whilst pretty nightingales
did sing melodiouslie.

Woods & mountaines,
& all yo^{w} weeping fountaines
assist my moanes:
my distressed trouble
let sad ecchoes double
with endles groanes.
Ô may ye spring bee here hence fled
& nothing nourish;
let no tree flourish

let violets
hang downe y^{r} dewy heades,
& be like her interr'd
within y^{r} earthly beds.

The third stanza bears favorable comparison with another anonymous lyric "Woods, Rocks, & Mountaynes, & ye desart places: (see my *Seventeenth-Century Songs and Lyrics*, University of Missouri Press, 1959, p. 478) extant in B.M. Add. MS. 11608, ff. 15^{v}-16 and also in the Bassus Book of this Carlisle Cathedral MS. — see Item 71 of the Bassus.

Item 74 This very popular lyric of Sir Robert Aytoun's is extant in several other MSS. (See "'Songs vnto the Violl and Lute' — Drexel MS. 4175," *Musica Disciplina*, XVI (1962), 73-92, item xiiii.) This manuscript version was of course unknown to Kenneth Elliott and Helena Mennie Shire in their *Song, Dance and Poetry of the Court of Scotland Under King James VI* (Cambridge University Press, 1969), [See FLIEP T.2249.]

Item 75 This is Robert Johnson's setting of the Battle of Pelusium from Fletcher's *The Mad Lover* which, hitherto, was known only from Drexel MS. 4041, ff. 24^{v}-26 (see: "Drexel Manuscript 4041: Earl Ferrers' MS. — a treasure-house of early Seventeenth-century song and dramatic lyric," *Musica Disciplina*, XVIII

(1964), 151-202. The setting is fully commented upon in "Music and *The Mad Lover*," *Studies in the Renaissance*, VIII (1961), 236-248.

Item 76 Printed in *Sportive Wit*, 1656, p. 41 and in several early eighteenth-century collections of songs. This item also occurs in Bodleian MS. Don. c. 57, f.41^{v} from which I edited it in *Seventeenth-Century Songs and Lyrics*. (University of Missouri Press, 1959), p. 396. There are the following variants from that text:

7 ere Noah's flood was] after Noah his flood being; [See FLIEP W.513, W.819.]

BASSUS BOOK

Commentary

The Commentary for the first 63 items is the same as above.

Bassus
Item 64 This occurs also in Bod. Lib. MS. Ch. Ch. Mus. 87, ff. 8^{v}-9 (see "'M^{ris} Elizabeth Dauenant 1624' Christ Church MS. Mus. 87," *RES*, X, 37 [February, 1959], 26-77) and in B. M. Add. MS. 24665, ff. 1-1^{v} from which latter MS. it was edited in Frederick Keele, ed. *Elizabethan Love Songs* (London, 1909), I. 93-5.

Bassus
Item 65 Michael Drayton's poem as set by Henry Bowman occurs also in Edin. Univ. Lib. MS. Dc.1.69, ff. 100^{v}-102 (see *Musica Disciplina*, XIII (1959), 169-194.) Henry Bowman included it in his collection of Songs for *1 2 & 3 Voyces*, 1677 (1678, 1679), p. 63. [See FLIEP G.384.] Brown printed this (p. 292) with no knowledge of Drayton's authorship.

Bassus
Item 66 Also by Michael Drayton — "To his Coy Love." It occurs also in Bodleian Lib. MS. Don. c.57, f. 49^{v} (see "A Bodleian Song-Book," *Music & Letters*, XXXIV, 3 [July, 1953], 192-212) and in Bodleian Lib. MS. Ch. Ch. Mus. 87, f. 12^{v} (see *RES*, X, 37 [February, 1959], 26-77.) [See FLIEP I.406.]

Bassus
Item 67 Brown printed this (p. 295) with his usual mixture of silent emendations; expansion of contractions; alteration to upper case, punctuation, etc.: that even if Brown's article were readily available, which of course it is not, it would be necessary to give the correct version.

> Away to ye fountaine you y^{t} will
> refine, refine, your Voices and yor skill,
> ye witts haue left it & are gone,
> 'tis now reserv'd for yo^{w} alone:
> and there is wine so rich, yow'l see
> each cup create new harmony, each :||: each :||:

each Voice, its equall height retaines,
in tuning here, in :||: you take no paines:
nor Violls nor ye Organs here,
but quarts & pottles may appeare, but quarts :||:
w^{c}h nee'r shall empty stand, there comes
no Eccho, there comes :||: from their hollow wombes,
from :||:
but fill'd w^{t}h mirth yor soules inspire.
seruing ye voice & witt much highe'r.

Then chant some catch & sing a round,
till emptied pipes till :||: your tunes resound, resound:
y^{t} smitten with yor powerfull art.
each God may come & beare a part, each God :||:

Brown printed the eighteen lines in three stanzas of six lines each, whereas it is quite clear in the manuscript that the poem is through-set and no divisions are suggestible until the change in tempo from ¢ to C3 at "Then chant." I have therefore printed it as divided this way.

Bassus
Item 68 The lyric occurs among the poems of Sir John Suckling, Poems 1646 and comes from IV.ii of his play *Aglaura*, King's Company of Players 1637. William Lawes' setting is fortunately extant in a complete version in Drexel MS. 4041, ff. 7-8 (see *Musica Disciplina*, XVIII (1964), 151-202) from which F. Rimbault edited it in *Musical Illustrations of Bishop Percy's Reliques of Ancient English Poetry* (London, 1850), pp. 82-3. It was much parodied (see G. F. Sensabaugh, "An Answer to Suckling's 'Why so' pale and wan, fond lover'" *MLN*, LII.6 (June, 1937), 410-411).
[See FLIEP W.2428 for further details.]

Bassus
Item 69 A version of this lyric is to be found in the Percy Folio MS., III.391, (see Robert Jamieson *Popular Ballads*, 2 vols., (Edinburgh, 1806), II.293-294; G. Neilson "A Bundle of Ballads," *Essays and Studies*, VII (1921), 108-142; and H. Grierson's *Donne's Poetical Works*, (Oxford, 1913), I. 452-453). It is extant also in another music MS., Drexel 4257, no. 234.

Great & proud, if shee deride mee,
let her goe, I'le neer despaire:
ere to morrow I'le provide mee,
one as great, lesse proud, more faire.

Those y^{t} seeke loue to constraine,
haue y^{r} labour for y^{r} paine.

Bassus
Item 70 Brown printed this item (p. 287) with no knowledge of its being Nicholas Breton's (see Hugh Macdonald, ed. *England's Helicon*, 1600, (Harvard, 1950), pp. 51-53. For a parody see "In a fair morn, O fairest morn, was euer morn so faire" *Wit's Interpreter*, 1655, Sig. H). Thomas Morley's setting of Breton was printed in Morley's *The first booke of Ayres*, 1600, as number xii.

Faire in a morne, ô fairest morne,
was neuer morne so faire:
w^{n} as ye sun, but not y^{t} sun
y^{t} shineth in ye aire.
& on a hill, ô fairest hill,
was neuer hill so blessed,
y^{r} stood a man, was neuer man,
for no man so distressed,
y^{r} stood a man, was neuer man,
for no man so distressed.

Bassus
Item 71 Robert Johnson's setting of these words has proved extant also in Bodleian Lib. MS. Don. C.57, f.6 (see *Music & Letters*, XXXIV, 3 [July, 1953], 192-212); Bodleian Library MS. Ch. Ch. Mus. 87, f.11 (see *RES*, X, 37 [February, 1959], 26-77), and in B.M. Add. MS. 11608, ff. 15^{v}-16 from which last manuscript I edited it in *Seventeenth Century Songs and Lyrics* (Missouri University Press, 1959), p. 428. There are the following variants from that text:

3 wth disgraces] w'h a thousand disgraces; 4 yo^{u}] yee;
6 woes while] woe; whilst

Only the first verse occurs here in the Carlisle MS.
[See FLIEP W.2781a which merely lists the Don. C.57 item.]

Bassus

Item 72 Printed between nos. 39 and 40 of Thomas Lodge's *Phillis* sonnetts, and also in the *Phoenix Nest*, 1593. John Ford's musical setting was printed in *Musicke of Sundrie Kindes*, 1607 as no. iv. The setting survives in the following music MSS. also: Adv. MS. 5.2.14 (Treble), ff. 21-21^{v}; Edinburgh University Lib. MS. 490, 73 (Treble); B.M. Add. MS. 24665, ff. 59-59^{v}. There are the following variants from the received text as given in *EMV*, pp. 470-471:

4 unconstant] inconstant; 8 plague] plunge*; 9 Of thine eye] Ô thine eyes; 13 that me aggrieved] w^{c}h me so greiued; 17 Feigned] Kind; 18 but] with; 19 trust] faith; 22 sorry] little; 25 O seemly] ô beauteous; 27 guide] gall.

*Clearly looks like "plunge" but seems very odd. In Bassus item 74 for instance, "The plagues of loue" looks exactly like "ye plunge of loue."

Verse 5 does not occur here in the Carlisle MS.

[See FLIEP N.503.]

Bassus

Item 73 I have not traced this item anywhere else.

O your louely sparkling eyes
o yor smiles betray mee,
while they with hopes delay mee.
Happier hee at once y^{t} dye's,
with your angrie eyeinge,
then thus still to bee dyeinge.

quickly sweet y^{n} kill,
or quickly saue mee:
order at yor will
ye life yo^{w} gaue mee.

Bassus

Item 74 This remarkably dramatic setting of a song from Fletcher's *The Mad Lover* is extant also in Edinburgh University Library MS. LA. III. 483, 200-1 (Bass only); Trinity Coll. Dub. MS. F. 5.13, ff. 30-31^{v} (Treble only); Fitzwilliam Museum MS. 52D 99^{v}-100. The first two MSS. were originally one. I edited the settings and included them in my *Musique de Scène* (Paris, 1959), 58-61, 155-156). There are the following variants from the 1647F, Sig. C4 text as given pp. 155-156:

1 deep's] depthes; 2 fond man the plagues] (fond man) ye plunge; 3 the] those... loves] ioyes; 6 Beloved againe, thou shalt see those ioyes never] & bin beloue'd againe, y^{u} come'st y^{r} neuer; 10 these] those; 11 They] those; 15 fires] fire; 16 desires] desire; 17 these] y^{r}... paines] paine.

The three versions, LA. III with F.513, 52D, Carlisle MS., make an extremely interesting study of *how* dramatic music may have been performed. There is obviously some attempt at vocalizing musical embellishments.

There is a mock of this song "Bacchus, I am come from the sun-shine fell" in *Merry Drollery Compleat*, 1691, p. 69.

Bassus

Item 75 I have made this item the subject of a separate study. The song belongs to Fletcher's *Beggars' Bush*. (See my "A newly discovered early seventeenth-century musical setting of 'Bring out your cony-skins, fair maides, to me' from Fletcher's *Beggars' Bush*," *Comparative Drama*, V, 2 (Summer, 1971), 101-105.